THE
HEART
OF
THE
UNIVERSITY

Originally Compiled by
Keith Denham and Alberto Yarza -
Revised by
Philip Opher

who thanks John Ashdown, Joanna Dodsworth,
Susie Geddes and Lucy Todd for their help

First published 1975
Revised 1991, 1994

HERITAGE TOURS PUBLICATION

1

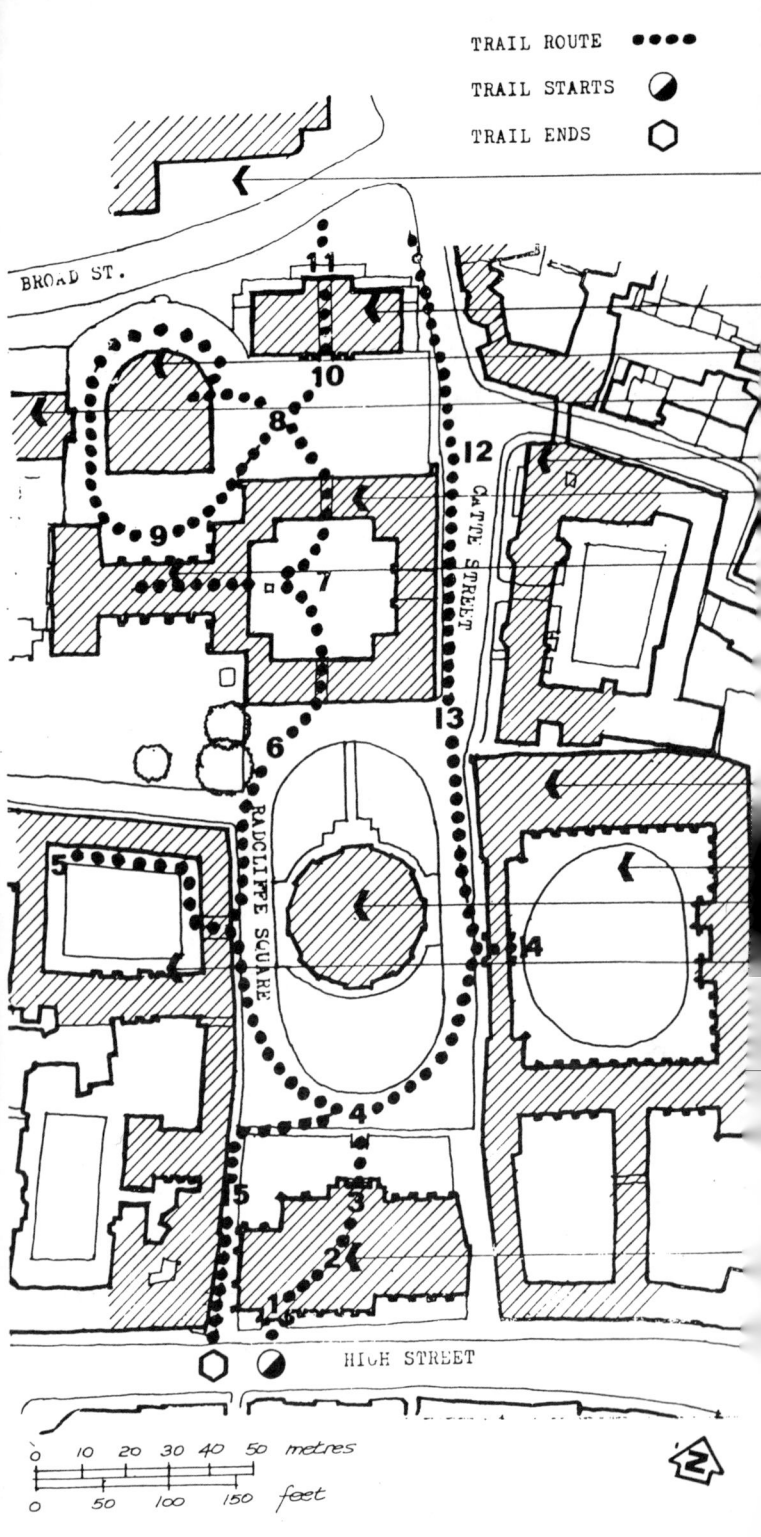

TRAIL ROUTE ●●●●
TRAIL STARTS ◐
TRAIL ENDS ⬡

BROAD ST.

11
10
8
9
12
7
CATTE STREET
6
13
RADCLIFFE SQUARE
5
4
5
3
2
1
HIGH STREET

0 10 20 30 40 50 metres
0 50 100 150 feet

N

_____ **New Bodleian Library**

_____ **Clarendon Building**

_____ **Sheldonian Theatre**

_____ **Old Ashmolean Museum**

_____ **Hertford College**

_____ **Schools and Old Bodleian**

_____ **Divinity School and Duke Humfrey's Library**

_____ **Codrington Library**

_____ **All Souls, North Quadrangle**

_____ **Radcliffe Camera**

_____ **Brasenose College**

_____ **St. Mary's Church**

The map on the previous pages shows a suggested route starting at St Mary's, the one on page 5 indicates the space between buildings which is normally accessible to the public.

INTRODUCTION

The University of OXFORD does not have a campus, its buildings are spread around the City. In most places College buildings predominate, but in one area, about 100 meters east of the commercial centre, there are a group of magnificent buildings which have always been the Heart of the University.

It was here in St Mary's Church, sometime about the middle of the 12th century that the university's governing body, the Congregation, first met, that the administration, the University Chest was carried out and the first degree ceremonies were held.

During the next two centuries the independent and self governing colleges, which supplied most of the students for the University, were founded and developed but it was not until 1320 that the first new building was provided for the University itself. This was a modest annex to St Mary's, now a delightful coffee shop, for the Chest and a small room above for the library. Another hundred years elapsed before the first independent building, the Divinity School with Duke Humfrey's Library above, were built and a further two hundred before the Schools Quadrangle and Convocation House completed this group. Degree ceremonies remained in St Mary's until Wren built the Sheldonian in 1669. The whole area was complete, largely as we see it today, with the construction of the Clarendon Building and the Radcliffe Camera around the beginning of the 18th century.

Four colleges, Brasenose, All Souls, Hertford and Exeter enclose the area and like the university buildings these have been added to and modified over the centuries. However one of the remarkable aspects of the area is its overall unity embracing a series of complex and varied urban spaces and a variety of building uses in various architectural styles. Thus the whole area is an excellent example of a typically English approach to urban design, formal without being strictly geometric, dignified without being ponderous and made up of buildings whose architects treat the strict rules of style in a delightfully free and relaxed way.

HIGH STREET

10 20 30 40 50 metres

feet

50 100 150

5

1. ST MARY'S CHURCH PORCH

The University Church of St Mary the Virgin, Oxford's Parish Church, is easily identified in the High St by its soaring spire, which dominates the scene. This spire, 46m (150ft) high, is probably the highest of any parish church in the country and is certainly one of the most beautiful. We will see it better from the far side of the church.

Before entering, have a look at the main porch, on the High St. This porch, built in 1637, is in the Baroque (meaning, literally, overwrought, florid, or extravagantly ornamented) style which was all the rage in Italy at the time when, after two hundred years, architects and their clients had become bored with the strict rules of the 'Classical' architecture of the early Renaissance. In England this kind of

The Baroque Porch of
St Mary's Church in the
High Street. 1637.
A style rarely found in England
especially applied to a Gothic
Church.

design was strikingly, and probably scandalously, new. The sensuously twisted Corinthian columns, the volutes, the broken pediment ending in scrolls, and the shell-topped niche above the statue of the Virgin with angels perched on either side must have shocked local people who had only recently become acquainted with the Renaissance from the few elements that were introduced half-heartedly into the Schools Quadrangle (7).

Everyone at the time would have known that this porch was directly inspired by the Canopy which Bernini had just had built over the high altar in the Pope's Church of St Peter in Rome. King Charles I had just bought a painting of it by Raphael (the Raphael cartoons now in the Victoria and Albert Museum in London). The Virgin's statue would have confirmed popular suspicion that this was a piece of Roman Catholic propaganda.

To illustrate how superficial popular local knowledge of the new type of architecture was, the ceiling of the porch is in fact a Gothic fan vault - Oxford had to wait another thirty years for its first fully-fledged Renaissance building, Wren's Sheldonian (8).

One of the most remarkable things about the porch is the way that it fits in with the rest of the church. Would we today feel confident enough to build a modern addition to a fine old building? Perhaps it fits so well because it was built of similar stone, which has mellowed over the years to become the same colour and texture as the rest of the building.

2. ST MARY'S CHURCH

Proceed through the porch and into the church.

Like most other English churches, St Mary's has been altered and enlarged many times. From the plan you can see that only the tower and spire date from the thirteenth century and that both the nave, its aisles and the chancel (or choir) behind the organ screen are fifteenth century.

Nineteenth-century architectural historians divided English Gothic into three periods: Early English

ST MARY'S CHURCH

The congregation house with library above was the first central building of the University

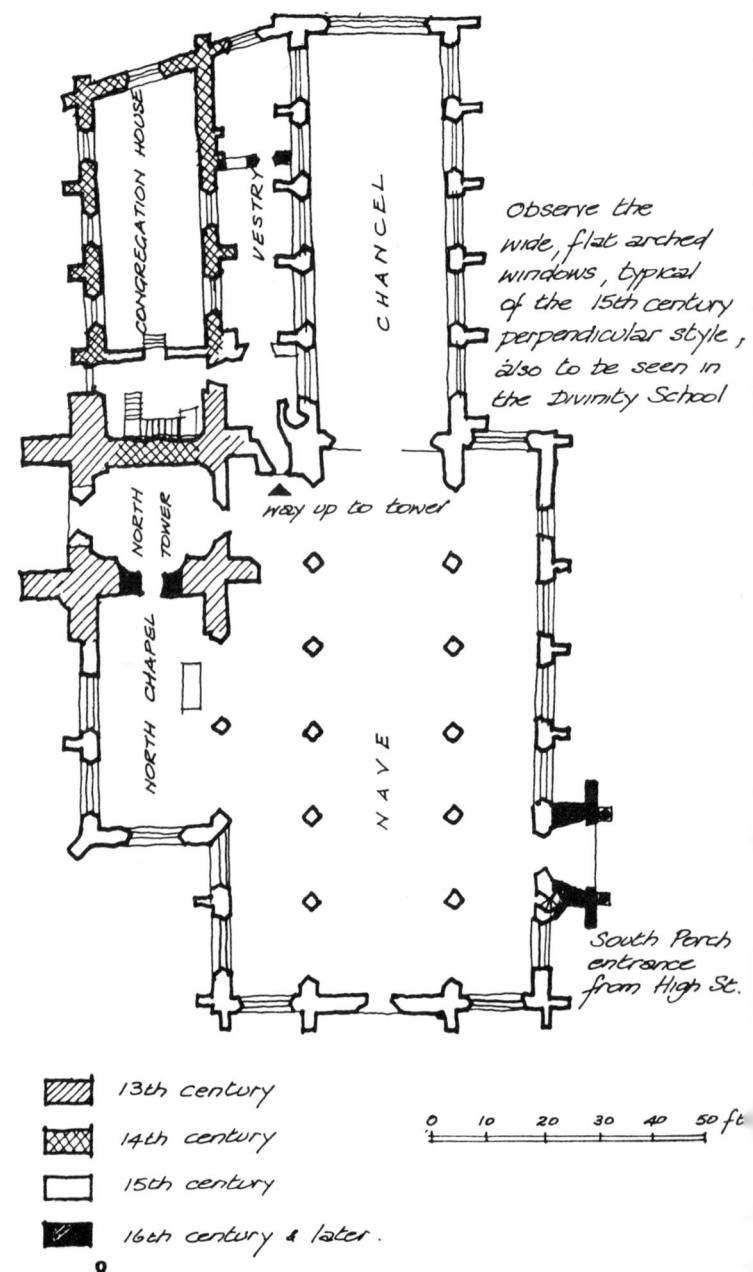

CONGREGATION HOUSE

VESTRY

CHANCEL

Observe the wide, flat arched windows, typical of the 15th century perpendicular style, also to be seen in the Divinity School

NORTH TOWER

▲ *way up to tower*

NORTH CHAPEL

NAVE

South Porch entrance from High St.

▨	13th century
▩	14th century
☐	15th century
◼	16th century & later.

0   10   20   30   40   50 ft

(1180-1300), Decorated (1300-1370), and Perpendicular (1370-1550) - St Mary's is a fine example of this latter style - tall, slender columns widely spaced, large windows, and an overall impression of lightness and delicacy.

In some churches and cathedrals the roof is a stone vault (see the fan vault in the porch and, later, the pendant vault in the Divinity School), but here we see a timber truss supported by stone corbels.

It was in this church that the University held its first meetings and ceremonies and it was here that the chests containing administrative documents and valuables were first kept.

Later, in 1320, a special room, known as the Congregation House, was built on to the north-east corner of the church and this, the first university building, served its purpose until 1534 when the administration moved to the west end of the Divinity School (7).

Above the Congregation Houses a room was built to accommodate the first library in England and this remained the only University library until 1488, when the Duke Humfrey's Library was built above the Divinity School. This library has now expanded into the world-famous Bodleian Library.

Apart from the pleasure derived from the delicate beauty of this interior and the admiration one might have for the skill of the stone masons and sculptors who constructed and decorated it, St Mary's, like many old buildings, gives us contact with historic people and with events from the past. At the foot of the last column in the nave you can still see where a platform was built from which, standing above the crowd, Thomas Cranmer was expected to recant his belief in the Reformation and to rejoin the Church of Rome. To the fury of his persecutors he changed his mind at the last moment and was taken straight from the church to be burnt at the stake in Broad St. The Martyrs' Memorial, erected at the southern end of St Giles in the late nineteenth century, commemorates the death , not only of Cranmer but also of Latimer and Ridley.

3. ST MARY'S CHURCH TOWER

We have already noted that the tower and spire of St Mary's is one of the tallest in England. If you look up from outside the north doorway you will see that it is very elaborate and beautiful, especially the four corners at the transition from tower to spire.

You can get a closer look at these if you go up the tower (entrance in the north porch fee £1.50) and, on a clear day, you can have one of the best views of Oxford. To ascend, enter through a small door, pass the old Congregation House and climb a wooden stair to an outside landing behind the tower.

From here you can examine the gargoyles and pinnacles of the nave roof at close quarters. Then continue by way of a narrow spiral staircase to the top.

From the outside gallery at the base of the spire the views are spectacular. Looking to the north and below you will see for the first time how the area where you will be walking is dominated by the magnificent Radcliffe Camera. Looking around you, note the form of the colleges, the unity provided by the stone, and the intrusion in some places of twentieth century buildings. But note also the predominance of green landscape which comes very close to the city centre. A whole book could be written about the views from this tower, so this guide will not elaborate upon this scene. Have a good look round, and particularly at the area of Radcliffe Square.

While you are up here, you should also take the opportunity to look down along the High St - often described as the most beautiful street in England. Looking east, you can see how it gently cures down to the tower of Magdalen College, past the famous sycamore tree on the left and Queens College beyond. To the west, where development is more concentrated towards the city centre, at Carfax (from the French *Carrefour* - crossroad) you can pick out the narrow plot divisions on the far side which were laid out in the early Middle Ages.

RADCLIFFE CAMERA

4. RADCLIFFE SQUARE

Descend the stairs and leave the church through the lobby of the north porch at the base of the tower and enter Radcliffe Square.

You may wish to pause for a while in the churchyard, to appreciate the sheer variety of buildings in this complex. To the left is the Chapel of Brasenose College, its large Gothic window with Gothic tracery, Classical surrounds, and some elaborate carving give an accent to the whole square. Next to the long library elevation, with its unusual Venetian Oriel window and beyond the gateway to Brasenose College you can see the high stone wall enclosing the garden of Exeter College.

The whole of the north side of the square is dominated by the Schools Quadrangle, with Catte St entering on the north-east corner. All Souls College fills the right side of the Square and, dominating the view is the massive circular form of the Radcliffe Camera (from the Latin *Camera* - room), 31m in diameter and rising 42m to the top of the dome - only slightly lower than the spire of St Mary's Church.

Radcliffe Square is considered to be one of the finest architectural compositions in England. It was conceived in the eighteenth century when all the buildings, except the Radcliffe Camera, were already in existence.

Dr Radcliffe, a famous physician associated with the University since his student days, bequeathed the money to found a library on his death in 1714.

Nicholas Hawksmoor took the opportunity to reconsider the whole area and give Oxford a fine public square (and a University Forum which was never built), to replace the haphazard jumble of medieval houses that originally filled the whole of this central area. It was also Hawksmoor who first suggested the idea of a circular library. However, seven years later, the trustees decided to hold an architectural competition, inviting Christopher Wren,

John Vanbrugh, James Gibbs, and Hawksmoor himself to submit plans. Only Hawksmoor and Gibbs did so, and fourteen years later Gibbs' design was selected in preference to Hawksmoor's. The foundation stone was laid in May 1737 and the building was finished after another twelve years, in 1749, thirty-five years after Dr Radcliffe's death! The building is now part of the Bodleian Library.

Gibbs' design, following Hawksmoor's lead, achieved one of the main ambitions of Renaissance architects - a free-standing circular building surmounted by a dome. The ground floor, built of wide-jointed stones, known as *rustication*, was originally an open-vaulted space, like a medieval market hall, used for informal meetings and discussions. It was not enclosed until the end of the nineteenth century.

The main two-storey rotunda in ringed with pairs of massive Corinthian columns just attached to the walls and topped by a deep cornice and balustrade decorated with stone balls where the Goths would have put pinnacles.

The building is entirely Classical and therefore unique in the square, yet it is in harmony with the buildings that surround it. Like the Baroque porch of St Mary's the use of the same type of stone provides a unifying element.

One of the reasons why the circular form is so satisfactory is that it solves a difficult urban design problem. Remember that when the building and square were planned there was a strong Classical tradition and it was considered important to have buildings centred on the axis of other buildings. However, the buildings around Radcliffe Square had been built in an earlier age when there were also houses obstructing the central space. No common axis could be established and therefore the circular shape resolves the problem by being non-directional. Its position in the centre, prevents one looking across the square and noticing the off-set position of the various entrances to the buildings.

The following illustrations are of various sculptures which can be found on buildings around Radcliffe Square that are described on this walk. You may wish to try and locate them as you continue.

HOLLAR'S MAP of 1643 (looking South) before Radcliffe Camera, Sheldonian and Clarendon Building were built.

Note how the monumental
scale of the Radcliffe Camera
and St Mary's Tower accentuates
the domestic character of
the college buildings.

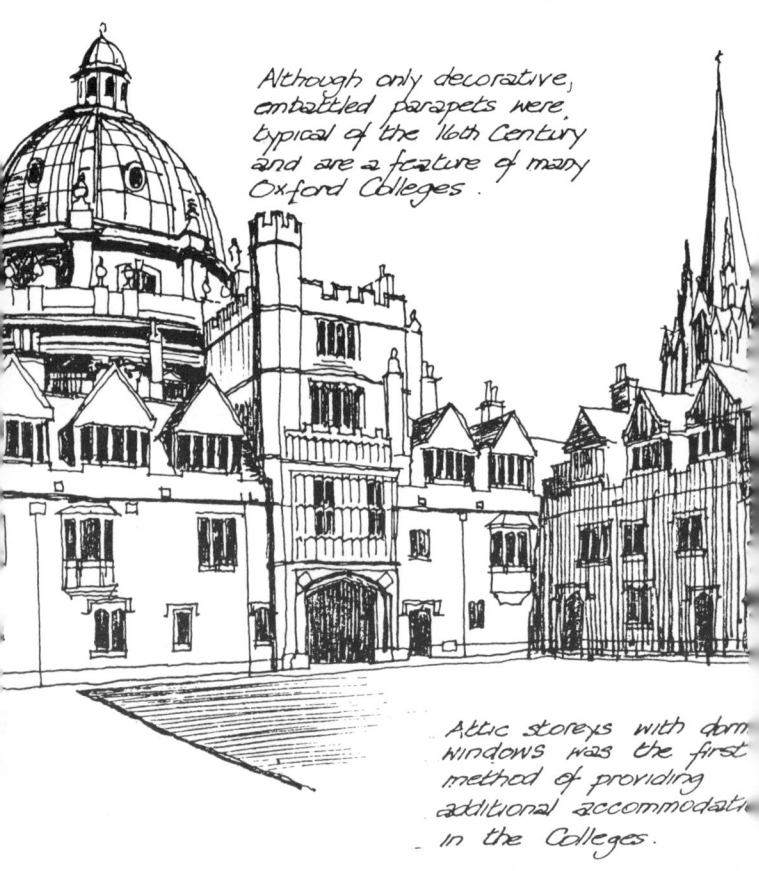

Although only decorative,
embattled parapets were
typical of the 16th Century
and are a feature of many
Oxford Colleges.

Attic storeys with dorm
windows was the first
method of providing
additional accommodati
in the Colleges.

5. BRASENOSE COLLEGE

Proceed to the west side of the square and enter the gateway of Brasenose College.

You may perhaps wonder at the name of this college, but if you look at the head of the great oak entrance doors you will see a bronze mask or 'brazen nose'. This feature was first mentioned in 1534. The first quadrangle was completed by about 1516, and altered about a hundred years later by the addition of the rooms in the roof with their dormer windows. This is typical of the method by which many of the Oxford colleges expanded their accommodation. Another typical feature of Oxford is the embattled or *crenellated* parapets seen on the entrance tower. This is an architectural detail of the tudor period, arising from the need to defend buildings in earlier times. The feature lingered on as a decorative motif and was revived by architects of the nineteenth-century Romantic movement.

Proceed to the north west corner of the quad. Look back at the huge dome of the Radcliffe Camera, looming over the entrance tower, with the spire of St Mary's to the right. This view emphasises the domestic scale of the typical college quadrangle.

If you have time, go and visit the inside of the chapel, the main east window of which we saw from Radcliffe Square. You will be amazed by the ceiling!

6. and 7. SCHOOLS QUADRANGLE and the DIVINITY SCHOOL

From Brasenose College, cross the north-west corner of the Square and proceed towards the Schools Quadrangle of the Bodleian Library.

You will find that much of Radcliffe Square is cobbled. The use of this material was very common in old streets, but, being unsuitable for the motor car, it has often been replaced by tarmac, as on the east side of the square. Flatter, square cobbles are known as *granite sets*, and the path towards the library is made up of these. Try walking on all the paving surfaces in Radcliffe Square and decide which you find the most satisfactory.

The Schools Quadrangle facing you was built in 1613. From the outside this is a remarkably plain, fortress-like block of Gothic masonry, topped with decorative pinnacles and crenellations. The only emphasis is the gateway facing Catte St but, even here the decoration is modest compared with that which we shall find inside. This was one of the first and remains one of the largest of the buildings of the University, and although neither grand nor ponderous it is suitably grave and calm.

Enter the arch on the south side and proceed through the tunnel under the building.

Inside, the quad is a delight. Taller and narrower than the usual residential quad, it is still light and open. It was built to house the various schools of the University, i.e. Geometry, Arithmetic, and Languages; Metaphysics; Logic; Grammar, History, and Moral Philosophy; Astronomy and Rhetoric; Music; and natural Philosophy, which are indicated over the various doors.

The inside of the quad is less austere than the outside. On the west side the walls are delicately panelled, and dominating the whole space is the remarkable entrance tower. This is one of Oxford's most spectacular architectural compositions, in a style which is both Classical and Gothic, a mixture known as 'Jacobean' after King James I, who sits in a circular niche in the fourth storey, below his family coat of arms.

This tower introduced students to the five orders of Classical and Renaissance architecture already fully mature in Italy and France but new in early seventeenth-century England. From bottom to top, we see Tuscan, Roman Doric, Ionic, Corinthian, and finally a composite of Corinthian and Ionic orders. These orders are all surrounded with Gothic carving and above them are gothic towers and pinnacles.

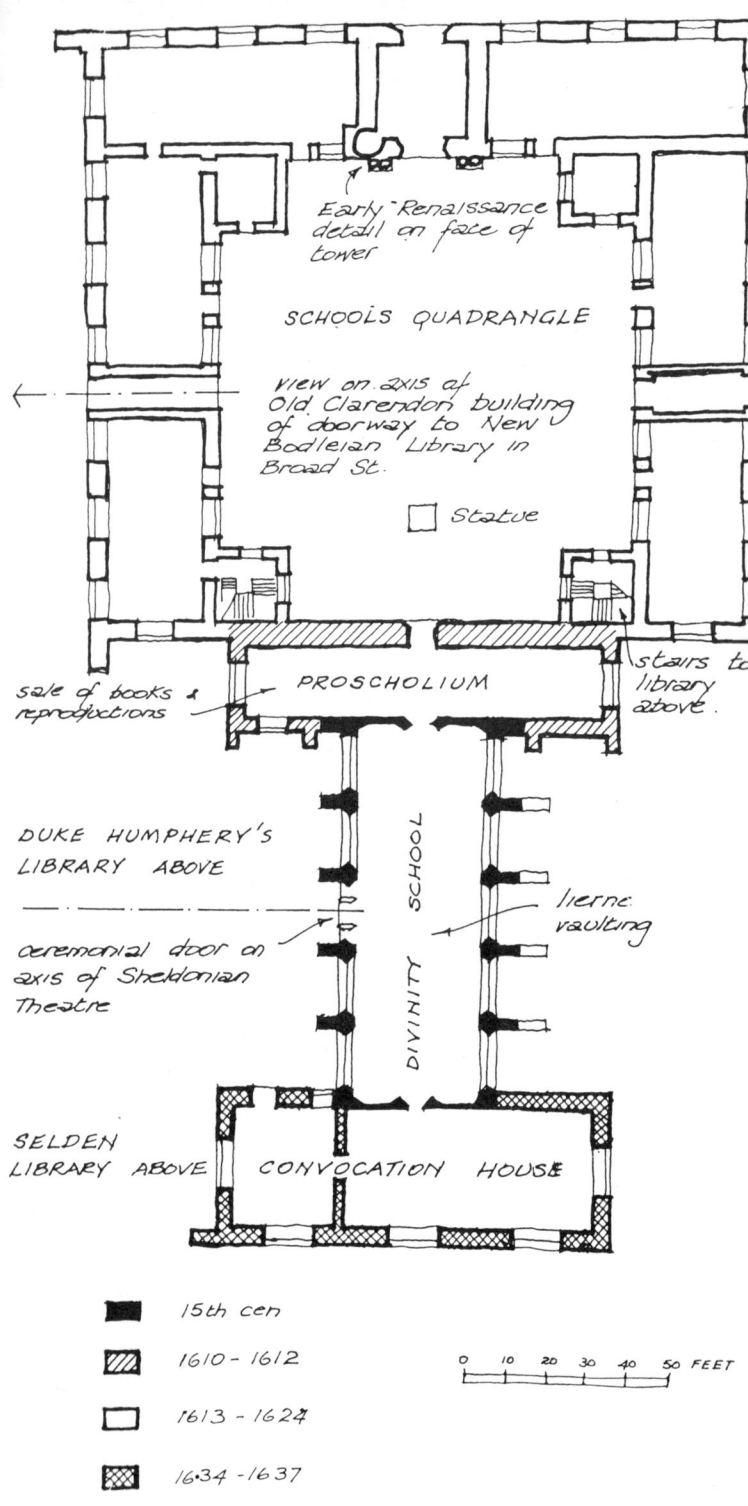

Early Renaissance detail on face of tower

SCHOOLS QUADRANGLE

View on axis at Old Clarendon building of doorway to New Bodleian Library in Broad St.

☐ Statue

sale of books & reproductions

PROSCHOLIUM

stairs to library above

DUKE HUMPHERY'S LIBRARY ABOVE

ceremonial door on axis of Sheldonian Theatre

lierne vaulting

DIVINITY SCHOOL

SELDEN LIBRARY ABOVE

CONVOCATION HOUSE

◼	15th cen
▨	1610 - 1612
☐	1613 - 1624
▦	1634 - 1637

0 10 20 30 40 50 FEET

The Quadrangle was built as an extension to the complex which housed the Divinity School, Duke Humfrey's Library, and the Convocation House for University meetings. You can see the original outside all of the Divinity School by walking behind the fine bronze statue of the Earl of Pembroke and into what is now the gift shop.

Straight on through another door, you enter the Divinity School proper. At first the building was designed as a single-storey, built between 1420 and 1483. Note the magnificent *lierne vaulting* with pendants. This vault, together with the large window, is typical of the period and is contemporary with the nave and chancel of St Mary's church. The vaulting supported the library which was built on top at a later date, after a bequest from Duke Humfrey.

Bearing in mind that the type of vaulting was the ultimate in the constructional skill of the Gothic builders, and considering the weight generated by a library, you will not be surprised to hear that the vaulting has been a continuing source of trouble. However, in recent years a new reinforced concrete floor has been added above it to support the library.

As far as we know, no one has ever counted the amazing number of bosses (which originated as the *key stone* of a vault) at the junction of every vaulting rib. These bosses are all elaborately decorated either with inscriptions each word being a separate boss - mostly in latin but including "thank God of al" (can you spot this?) or with Coats of Arms or monograms. Many of these are of Thomas and John Kemp - Bishop of London and Archbishop of Canterbury or of William Waynflete, who founded Magdalen College, but they also include "W.O." possibly those of the architect of the building William Orchard.

Unfortunately Duke Humfrey's library is now only open for scholars except for guided tours at certain times and so we must go outside again and leave through the arch on the north side of the Schools Quadrangle.

THE SHELDONIAN THEATRE

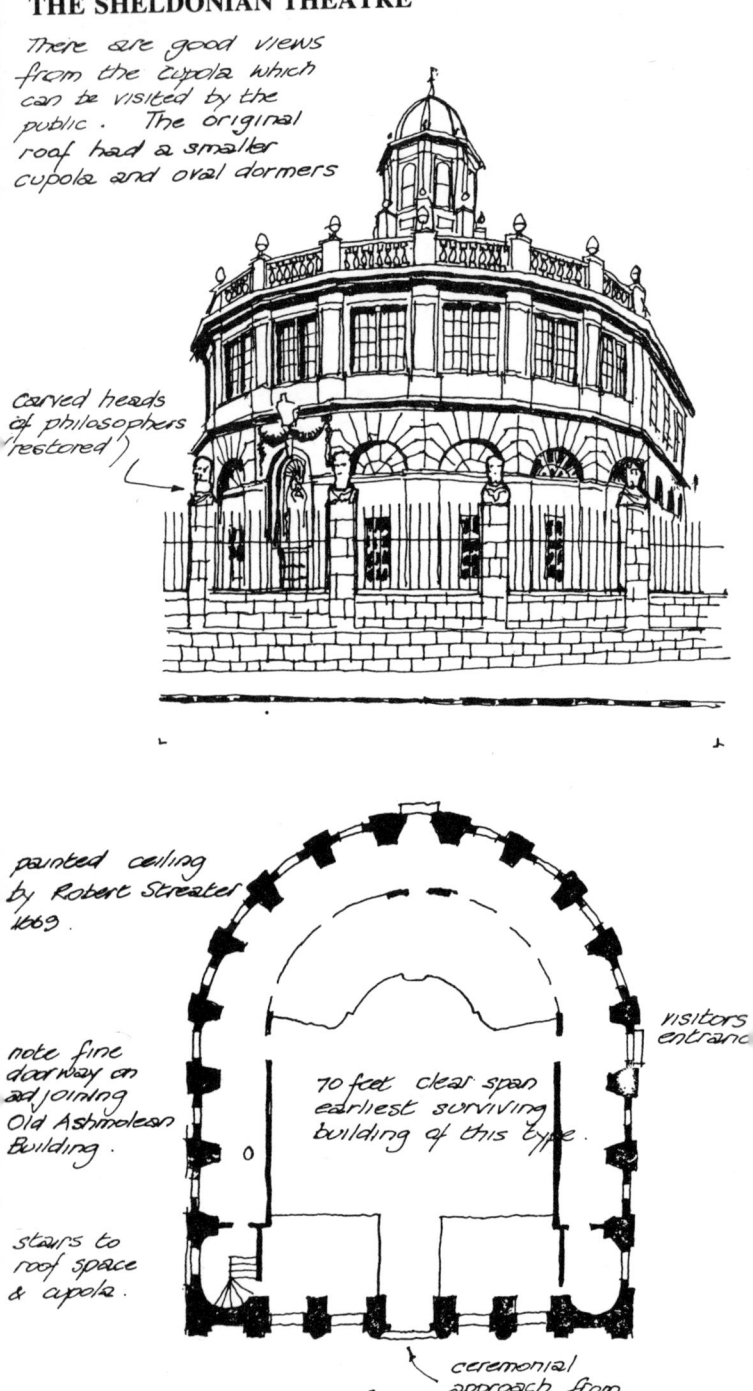

There are good views from the cupola which can be visited by the public. The original roof had a smaller cupola and oval dormers

Carved heads of philosophers (restored)

painted ceiling by Robert Streater 1669.

note fine doorway on adjoining Old Ashmolean Building.

stairs to roof space & cupola.

visitors entrance

70 feet clear span earliest surviving building of this type.

ceremonial approach from Divinity School.

0   10   20   30   40   50 feet

8. THE SHELDONIAN

You have now arrived in a complex open space. The building on the left is the Sheldonian Theatre, an assembly hall for the *Encaenia*, the ceremonial confirming of University degrees, and that directly ahead is the Clarendon Building. You will note that these are in a different style from the buildings you have already seen round Radcliffe Square, except for the Radcliffe Camera. They are, of course, of later date. The Sheldonian was built between 1664 and 1669, and the Clarendon Building between 1711 and 1713, when the Renaissance had become firmly established in England. The Sheldonian was one of Christopher Wren's first designs and is the earliest surviving structure of its kind in England. It is 70 ft wide, with no intermediate supports. At certain times there is public access to the *cupola*; the views are similar to those from St Mary's. In the roof space, through which one passes to reach the cupola, the huge timber trusses necessary to span the space below are in full view.

Since the Sheldonian was built for University ceremonies the principal participants would proceed from the Convocation House at the far end of the Divinity School. The main entrance façade of the building has therefore to turn its back on the public street. Wren's and Oxford's revolutionary classical composition is thus almost hidden away, to the relief of some critics who find the way its giant pilasters break into the pediment a rather amateur first attempt at design. Wren was in fact, Professor of Astronomy at the time!

The rest of the building, based on a drawing in a book by an Italian called Serlio, who in turn got his ideas from a Roman theatre, is less formal, with the back sticking out into Broad St like the stern of a ship. Architects to this day have trouble designing the backs of buildings - just look at the back of your local supermarket!

Incidentally, Wren almost certainly designed the new doorway (9) from the Divinity School, in a very respectable Gothic.

To the west of the Sheldonian, and started a few years later, is the old Ashmolean Museum. Facing Broad Street, the building is like a typical large house of the period, although there are only one or two of these in Oxford. There is a richly carved ceremonial doorway facing the theatre. This doorway, with its circular pediment, should be compared with the entrance to St Mary's (1) to illustrate how varied Renaissance design can be.

ASHMOLEAN MUSEUM.

10. THE CLARENDON BUILDING

The final building we come to in this University complex is the Clarendon Building, erected in 1713 for and by Oxford University Press for their printing works, which had outgrown its first home in the basement and roofspace of the Sheldonian.

Lord Clarendon, after whom the building is named wrote the *History of the Great Rebellion*. The Press paid for the building out of the profits it made from this eighteenth-century bestseller, and remained here until the end of the nineteenth century. The building is now the Registry of the University but OUP books are still published under the 'Clarendon' imprint!

Nicholas Hawksmoor produced the design while working at Blenheim Palace under his teacher (and later partner) Sir John Vanbrugh. (Vanbrugh's epitaph was 'Lie heavy on him earth for he hath laid many a heavy load on thee'). Looking at the Clarendon Building, it is obvious that Hawksmoor was a good pupil.

The two main elevations of the building both have huge Tuscan columns, rising through both storeys and supporting a pediment. On the Broad St side these columns stand free of the building on top of a flight of steps, creating a massive entrance portico to the group of buildings to the south. On the south elevation similar columns are attached to the building. All the details particularly the deeply recessed windows are heavy and largely undecorated, in sombre contrast to those of the surrounding buildings. Although with none of the frivolity of the Italian Baroque, which we saw on the porch of St Mary's (1), Vanbrugh's and Hawksmoor's buildings are regarded as a English version of the Baroque style.

Perhaps you find the delicacy of the fine wrought iron gates, which close off the passage that passes through the building, more to your taste.

11-12 SERIAL VISION-CATTE STREET

So far on this walk we have been looking at buildings as if they stood in isolation, but in fact towns are made up of collections of buildings, usually seen while moving past them. The arrangement of buildings in towns is sometimes called *townscape*, the art of ensemble, experienced with *serial vision*.

You might like to retrace your steps from the Clarendon Building through the Schools Quadrangle and out into Radcliffe Square, noticing the ever-changing relationship of yourself to the buildings, and of the buildings to each other.

Alternatively, you can go into Catte Street to the east and take the route described by Thomas Sharp, the Oxford planner who first defined townscape in his book *Oxford Replanned* published in 1948. Sharp wrote:

> "As we approach the Bodleian from Catte Street there is nothing to be seen but its noble cube. Advancing we see first the Rotunda, then the spire of St Mary's, then the dome of the Radcliffe coming into view. As this vast circular bulk separates from the Bodleian, the tower of St Mary's also emerges. Despite the fact that each of these three buildings is in its own way as sophisticated a piece of architecture as there is, the experience is elemental beyond the power of words or photographs to describe. Cube, cylinder and cone are suddenly juxtaposed, or rather suddenly deploy, the one from the other with a result that is architecturally speaking sensational."

Walking along Catte Street you may have noticed several unusual buildings on your left: On the corner the former Indian Institute, in a pleasing mixture of Oriental Baroque on the rounded corner and Jacobean on the rest (don't miss the delightful line of carved elephants). Further along there is an octagonal chapel with a steep pointed roof which is the only medieval building on this side of the street. More surprising is an anglicised copy of the famous Bridge of Sighs in Venice, here linking the two parts of Hertford College across New College Lane. The bridge (built in 1913) and the other buildings of the college, in various architectural styles - Palladian Jacobean on the left, and Classical on the right - were all designed by the very prolific late nineteenth-century Oxford architect Thomas Jackson who fired shots in several directions in the battle of styles which was then at its height and which so disgusted the puritanical twentieth-century architects of the Modern Movement.

14. ALL SOULS COLLEGE

Back in Radcliffe Square again we have not yet looked at the east side, occupied by All Souls College, a graduate college which dates back to 1438. The oldest, South Quadrangle, is entered from the High St. You may be surprised to learn that the North Quadrangle was designed by Nicholas Hawksmoor, turning his hand, like Wren had before him, to the 'Gothick' when he thought it appropriate. He took the opportunity to consider the design in the context of his plans for Radcliffe Square as a whole. It was in fact his only opportunity to influence the buildings surrounding the Square and he had to take into account the existing chapel. The result is an extremely original design which combines Classical symmetry with Gothic detail. The west side of the quadrangle facing Radcliffe Square is merely a covered colonnade. However, it remains very important in defining the space. How often today are architects allowed to use such a device without providing usable space?

The building on the north side of the quadrangle is the Codrington Library, which, although it was begun in 1716 but is externally Perpendicular Gothic in design complete with crenellations and pinnacles, matching the chapel at the other end of the colonnade. How does this compare with the accepted date of the Perpendicular style? However, if you look behind the 'Gothick' tracery of the big window in the library you can just see the silhouette of a Venetian window, a favourite Renaissance motif, on the inside. Thus Hawksmoor literally had it both ways - Gothic outside, Classical in - a case of hedging the architectural bets.

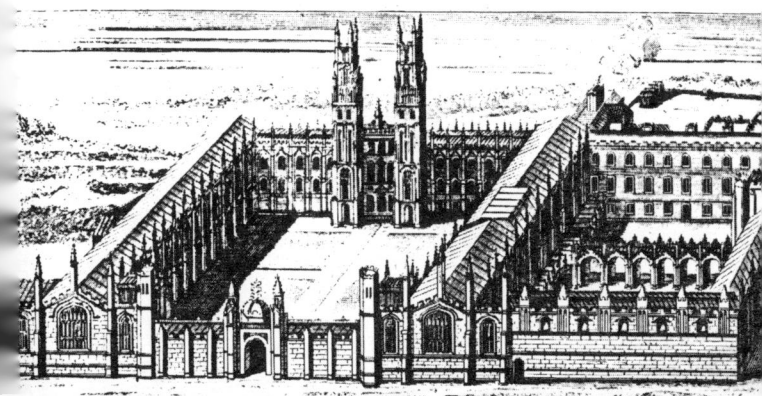

ALL SOULS COLLEGE

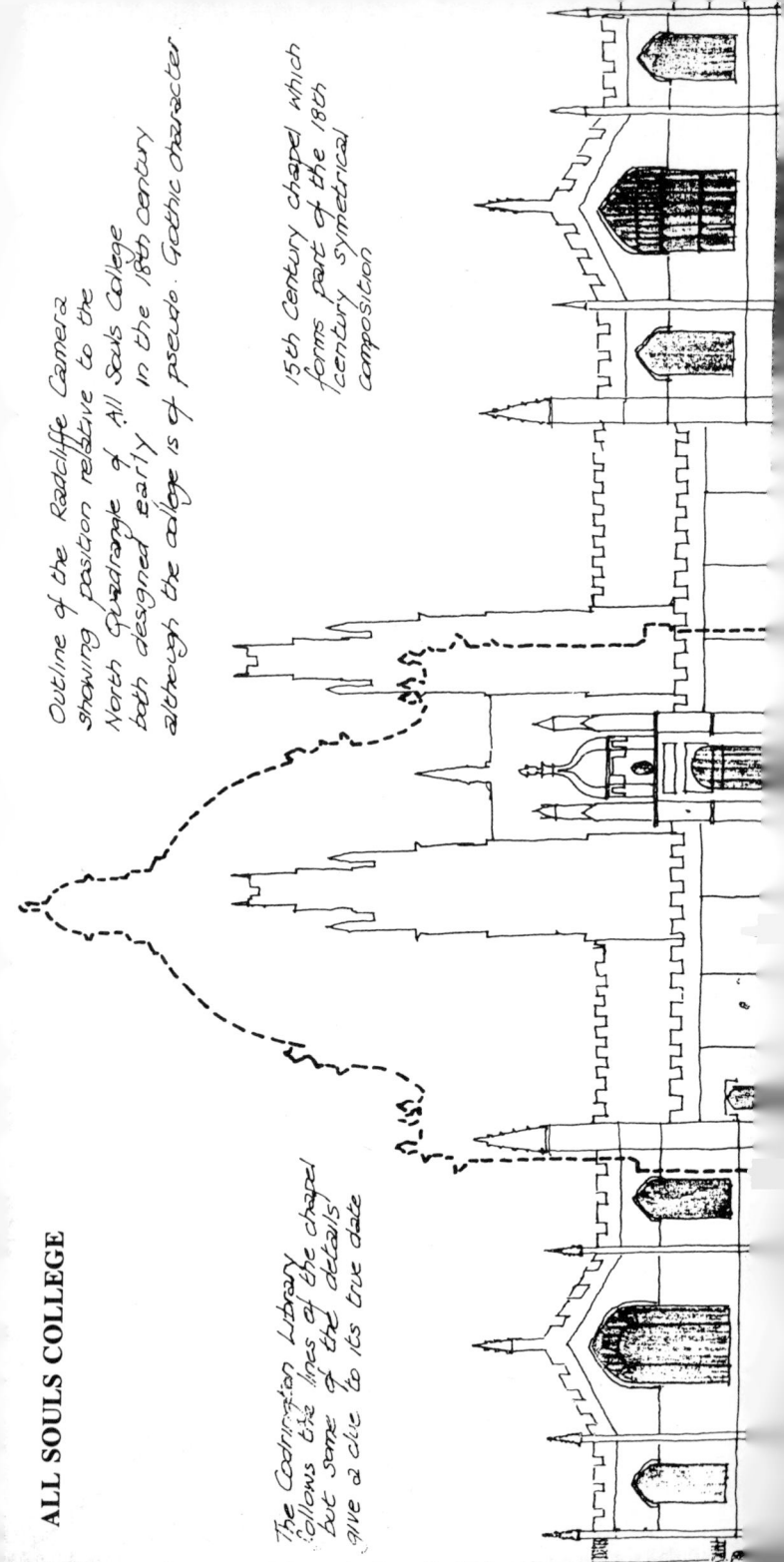

Outline of the Radcliffe Camera showing position relative to the North Quadrangle of All Souls College both designed early in the 18th century although the college is of pseudo. Gothic character

15th Century chapel which forms part of the 18th century symetrical composition

The Codrington Library follows the lines of the chapel but some of the details give a clue to its true date

We are now nearing the end of the walk and, to return to our starting-point, we cross the square to the passage (15) on the west side of St Mary's.

Along this passage are the only remaining houses in the area. Note how complicated and diverse the fronts of these houses have become as a result of the alterations which have taken place over the years. The details are Victorian but the buildings are sixteenth century in origin. Radcliffe Square was once filled with houses like these, which is not quite difficult to believe. It is also difficult to believe that a few year ago Radcliffe Square was a busy through route for traffic. we should be grateful to the City Engineer for the opportunity to walk round in comparative peace and quiet.

This walk, which has taken us through one of the great urban places of Europe, ends where it started - in the High St. You have seen several fine buildings, of different architectural styles, brought together in an outstanding townscape. You may well have seen these buildings before, in photographs or drawings, but you have now experienced them in their totality - space, light, sound, colour and movement. This is the only way to enjoy architecture since no photographs or drawings can capture its complex qualities and relationships, nor can they capture the thrill of 'being there'.

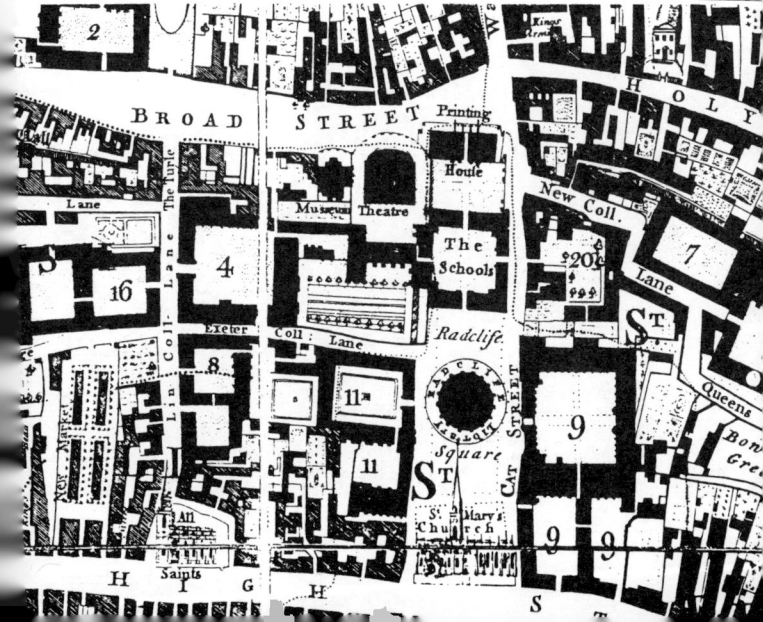